Dignity

Dignity

*Challenges to the Inherent Dignity of the
Human Person and the Sanctity of Human Life*

ANITA M. HESSENAUER

RESOURCE *Publications* · Eugene, Oregon

DIGNITY
Challenges to the Inherent Dignity of the Human Person and the Sanctity
of Human Life

Resource Publications
An Imprint of Wipf and Stock Publishers
199 W. 8th Ave., Suite 3
Eugene, OR 97401

www.wipfandstock.com

PAPERBACK ISBN: 979-8-3852-5196-4
HARDCOVER ISBN: 979-8-3852-5197-1
EBOOK ISBN: 979-8-3852-5198-8
VERSION NUMBER 02/23/26

In honor of those who have the insight to recognize the divine
in all human persons and who labor tirelessly to uphold the
dignity of the human person.

CONTENTS

TO DEHUMANIZE

THE DEHUMANIZATION OF INDIVIDUALS or of peoples within a particular race or religion has been a scourge dotting human history throughout the ages. This poetry collection is a tribute to those known and little-known figures who have spent their lives and have given themselves in defense of the most vulnerable and those in the throes of extreme marginalization in our society and around the world. These figures understood that every individual is made in the image and likeness of the Creator and must be treated with dignity, love and respect for human life.

We live in a period of moral relativism, in which absolute values are scoffed at, suppressed or shunned. The autonomy of individual thought and way of life is the norm of our day. This is the moral compass by which we live our daily lives. Our original identity as children of the one Maker has been eclipsed and has very little or no place in our society or culture. It is not surprising that our lives are lived out according to our individual desires, opinions, likes and dislikes. In an egotistical sphere where the "self" is elevated, there is little or no room for the "other," and the concept of humankind as emanating from the divine is obliterated.

Linguistic terms used as greetings in diverse cultures, originated in the recognition of the presence of the divine in the "other." The Hindu greeting, *Namaste,* in its literal translation means "I bow to the divine in you." "Shalom" in Judaism connotes a deeper meaning of abiding peace and wholeness, which can only be given by our Creator. "Adieu," the farewell expression in French, shows the trust placed in the protection and care of our Supreme

Maker. Today, however, the original and deeper meaning of these terms, of which I've named only a few, seem to have lost their association with the divine.

This poetic collection also addresses some of the reasons for the dehumanization of the human person, such as racial superiority, hatred towards those not belonging to a certain religion or ethnicity, egotism, and sheer prejudice borne out through the generations. This *weltanschauung* of deep disrespect for the inherent dignity of the human person and the sanctity of human life, is visible in every arena of life. This collection is an attempt to make the reader aware of the great reach of a relativistic perspective on life, as well as to highlight those whose self-sacrificing and self-emptying love or *kenosis,* played and continues to play a large role in restoring the inherent dignity of the human person.

A world in which human life
is not measured by its utilitarian use

A life of self-emptying love -
Giving of oneself for another

During one of the most horrific periods of the twentieth century, the genocide of the Jewish people under Nazi Germany during World War II, Titus Brandsma, a Catholic priest belonging to the Carmelite Order, spent his last days in the Dachau concentration camp providing succor, support and hope to his fellow inmates who had succumbed to despair and hopelessness at the hands of their Nazi persecutors. Titus lifted the minds and hearts of countless victims of the Holocaust.

SACRIFICE

After Titus Brandsma

Reign of steel slicing into vulnerability,
Into the wound of listless breath.
A Spartan infusing warmth
into hollowed limbs laid waste, before the naked sheet of piercing
daggers.
The leathered soul swallows the elemental battery preying
on bodily fragility. Felled trees bare their entrails, offer their
precious cup of life . . .

The igneous brand inundates the expanse, readied to decimate;
Uncoils the staggering on swaying trunks.
Contagion of a smoldering wick, an impervious will,
Setting off a wildfire raging through
The desiccated boughs of dancing specters.

The scythe mows down, the willow bends,
The wind unleashes its weaponry on the scarred back of the
wheat.
The skin is peeled to the baldness of shaved cheese,

The water beats its staccato march, digs its heels into translucent
flesh,
Powerlessness – Surrender to the vengeful offering of the
waterfall.
The gaping throat swims in and out of consciousness.
The molten branding the swastika.
The flagellation of the P-38.
Myopic, blistered lives,
Drowning in the cauldron of the fatherland
Clicking the heels to the Fuhrer.

Shrinking of iron shod boots into guttural space.
The withered hands of Aryan supremacy
Oblivious to the mystery
Of the inner presence.

Untiring Resolve

A staunch belief in the inherent dignity of the human person, led
to the arrest of Nargis Mohammadi, an Iranian Journalist and
Human Rights Activist, condemned to life in prison.
Mohammadi won the Nobel Peace Prize in 2024 for her endless
struggle for the emancipation of Iranian women under the
regime of the Ayatollah and for her work in promoting human
rights and freedom for all.

CONVICTION

After Narges Mohammadi

The clouds float by, take the shapes of all I've dreamt of –
The greening of the valleys lights up a spark in my heart, barred
in a
window of dank walls, snuffed out by screaming bars.
The acute sense of warmth rises through the clipped wings of
arteries, veins and capillaries,
Refusing to let my eyes waft into an unknown sleep.

I chew on air . . .

A spark lights up in my heart -
Why do I hold on to the cloud,
Never letting it rain down?
Quelling the seed as it sprouts without showing off
its dress of verdant green,
Scorched into an ashen heap.

I run my callused hands over the clouds of touch -
Husband, children, parents -
Morphed into phantoms dredged out of seas long lost . . .
The solitude of walls coagulates into
Arrogant eyes that mock.
The bearded and turbaned Ayatollah dismisses
with a flick of the finger,
The insect caught in its own trap –
clinging to the rancid corner,
stuck to the porous crack into which it longs to disappear.
A body alienated from a mind on fire.
My heart strikes a spark.
The valleys, blanketed with the greening of oil rigs.

The cactus blooms in the furnace, combustion for the brain,
fuel for neurons.

A sea of uncovered heads sends its waves into the streets,
rising in incantations of flowing hair,
Lights a spark within my innermost chamber.
Wait, the air is hushed.
Syllables unspoken, meander in and out of shadowed walls,
carrying within the weight of death.

The breath of billowing clouds spews the unvoiced destinies
of the lost but not forgotten, now churned into the printing press.
Clandestine fecundity bursts the dykes of "white torture,"
Soaked in the presence of unapproachable light.
80 lashes reverberate in drenched silence,
Cornucopia of emptiness, plying the Stygian waters,
greening the valleys with ashen sparks.

I collect the embers of my heart.

A BROKEN BACK

Exasperation, taut on cords hung out to dry. Mother's chorus
rolls off her tongue. She's a pro at this! "*The boy needs to be in
school! Aray Bala, you're here again with Aaji? The school room
is where he belongs, Laxmi!*" She opens her arms wide, ready to
scoop up the ten-year-old, whose shaved head quickly disappears
into the fronds of the broom. He sweeps the room in meticulous
silence. "*Bai,*" Laxmi whispers, "*you might as well be talking
to a stone-deaf wall! His mind is afloat in distant skies.*"

Sapped bones, extinguished lights, sunken craters,
a promontory of yellowing and darkened decay. Laxmi squints back,
eyes shrouded with the lashes of time; a body buried under
an iron mantle, digging into sparse shoulders. Air whistling
through the aperture of interstices, she mutters raspingly,
"*a mind afloat in distant skies.*"

Dreams hung on the thorns of the *Babul,* burst without a touch,
carrying in their wake, the odor of festering hope and buried
ambition for this frail baby, offered to the vapors of a tropical
noonday sun. Laxmi dug ditches, cleared the baked earth for the
pipeline that was to bring clean water to the villagers. The oldest
among the laborers, age slapped her in the face, a cruel daily
reminder of her mortality. Fissures bored into the soles of her
bare feet, crisscrossed *wadis* of volcanic steam pushing through
a torrid world. Her nine-yard sari refused to provide solace to her
grieving legs, mourning the unearthed dirt lost in the darkness of
the quarry.

The baby, born of silence, child of the desiccating sun, eyes wide,
pupils dark, waits . . . for the milk of shriveled breasts.
Her daughter gone; she took on the role of mother.

His father abandoned the family; left for that big city, Mumbai.
Big brother, she said, was kidnapped by that slick man, hair
greased, film-star clothes, a breed apart from the fish in her

pond. *He's begging for his boss. That's what they do with the
children from the village . . . maim and use . . . Moola, moola, my
brother's making so much moola. That's where I must go! Bandya's*
daily refrain!

The bead glistens as it makes its arduous pilgrimage down her
forehead, reflecting in its salt waters, the rupees she could be
earning in that big city of promise. And what a promise! The
boy's father's dream of owning a taxi, now dissipated into the
life of a leashed dog, surviving to fill the pockets of the Mumbai
mafia

Selfishness and self-absorption wag their forked tongue at Laxmi;
dog her in moments of despair. *"Do what's good for you, take the
easy way out! Why worry about the boy? Think about yourself!"*
She had journeyed to the big city, she had seen *Bandya's* father
and brother, pitiable blind beggars, crying out to the bevy of
tourists in Bandra.

She returned to the village with *Bandya.* She made a pact with
herself - *I will not let the boy go! I know too much about that big
city. I will fight to the last and with spent breath, I will protect him.*

A broken back, a twisted torso, unpliable hands, hold the boy
in a caged embrace.

A stone-deaf wall, a cloud afloat in distant skies.

GRIT

Jolted into reality, the dawning of sunrise, soaking the platform
in gold, breaks open the dark secret to which she's clung
as treasure never to be lost.

What she had done, unimaginable to those left behind,
was now clearly delineated by the shrill whistle of the train
she had just boarded. It seemed like a dream, an eternity . . .
was it the present?

Tears well up, spilling uncontrollably onto what was once
a flawless terrain, now overgrown with the scars of silent abuse.
Slowly and deliberately, she runs her long, well- shaped fingers
over the bumps in the road, tracing every abscessed marsh,
ignited, and left to rot in the putrid story from which
she's struggling to escape. Where would she go, what would she
do? Alone, without a soul she could open up to. She cowers in
the wooden seat, the one furthest from the others, the one tucked
into the corner, shielded from nosy passengers or so she thinks.
The gray haired woman, hardened in the face, snarls at her from
across the way. She's caught in the act
of breaking free, like a dog on the run from its master, afraid,
despite its newly found freedom. And isn't that what she's doing?
The compartment filled with passengers compacted like tightly
packed sardines, she breathes the odor of fear
rising from her entrails. The piece of paper tucked into the blouse
of her sari is her only saving grace. An address in *Mahad*. *"Go
there!" The woman in red had told her at the well. "Go there! The
kind women will not convert you!" I will lead you where you should
go.*
There's no turning back now. It's a done deal! Look to the future . . .
The voice inside her was unmistakably clear.

How is it that our lives once upended can take on purpose,
magnetically drawing us toward the definitive mount
which must be scaled? Those dark moments of paralysis now
dripping water from the arctic glacier as we move away from
what was the axis of slipping time.

It was the appointment in the mobile medical van.
The turning point came with the steady beat of the machine.
She saw *her* on the monitor. She knew this was a life; tied
inextricably to hers.
Her head spun into a landslide of emotions, punching her
where it hurt the most. How could *Aai Sahib*?
How could *Baba* demand that she get rid of the baby?
Their insistence; their threats that she divests herself
from this burden. Why? Why? Because the baby was a girl!
She felt no shame.
Instead, peace washed over her – Shanti, as was her name.

The decision is implanted, the intricate workings of the human
mind and body in tandem, accomplices in the same endeavor.
The well-worn scrap of paper, now a salve.

A will cemented into a listening heart and a convergent soul, fuel
the locomotive to its destination.

DECISION

She hears the breathing. Her heart is impaled to the floor.
Why the contorted look on the physician's face?
The tightening of lips, a hardening of the jaws.
Silence hangs low, smothering all speech
with a giant sweep of its paw. The ominous sound. It's the
breathing . . .
She remembers the day. She remembers the scan. Yes, she was too
old!
The look that said, *can you afford this child? Are you ready to
carry this burden, be weighed down for a lifetime of unimaginable
hardship?* The length of the interrogation, derision and disdain
nailed into the
coffin
of
mind and heart.
She walked away, stalked by silence. He stood erect,
shaking his head in disbelief.
An extra chromosome, washed away with no vestige.
Now, she celebrates life.

St. Teresa of Calcutta is characterized by the way in which she treated every human person with the dignity they deserve. Through her unalterable love and compassion, she showed them their inherent worth and value. Those abandoned by family and friends found love and acceptance for the very first time with this great twentieth-century saint.

MY BODY FOR YOU

In the cradle of your arms, you held me; with utmost gentleness you rocked me, a skeletal babe. Your warmth, a heavenly infusion into a maggot infested carcass, withering in defunct, sickly sweet fumes. I am intricately woven into decay, one with the waste festering in dank heaps; married to filth. I am the stench you dare not approach.

How did you find me? Why did your uncalloused hands lift me out of the squalor I'm grafted onto? why? The nagging question . . .

My nothingness fades into nebulous silence; the steady, burial march of physicality, my only permanence. *Who am I?* Defined by the withered twigs in putrescent filth, osmotically one with rodent and pest. I float into a cavernous void.
The sow tucks her pillowed head against a shriveled cranium; these hollowed limbs warm within the blanket of her scaly bristles. The meticulous cleansing from the strays, an antiseptic for my sores. Their serum, an everlasting bond with my canine benefactors.
My eyes, marbled slates, drown in a waterfall that floods a dry land whose gluttonous mouth slurps the drops of this unknown commodity, in a country of endless drought. The gnawing on limbs, ready to ignite within these noxious fumes arouses the raging fury of the Gods. I am at their mercy.

Now, you hold me, an abomination. You refuse to let these dry bones go . . . Floating on the brink of consciousness, I hear the unthinkable -

"You are the beloved." The oozing of my open sores sings out the refrain. I am the beloved.

Sacred words inscribed on the parched story
of my non-existence. Moksha . . . Moksha!

Hate obliterates Life

The ongoing wars in the Middle East, Ukraine and around the world, witness to the countless and senseless loss of life.

BOILING POINT

When hate boils over, the world sinks into ashes.

Pythonic tentacles of molten lava strangle in one gigantic swoop,
asphyxiating and annihilating with a fiery tongue. It transcends
the desert, infiltrates the borders, lays bare the nations.

When hate boils over, its poison floods the oceans,
saturates the seas, overpowers the rivers,
the waterways, the canals, the roadways, the streets, and every

pore and cell lay steeped in its burn . . . It gallops up mountains,
burns hills, razes valleys, destroys plains, sparing nothing
with its caustic bite.

When hate boils over, it invades minds, explodes bodies.
It kills - thousands of miles away,
to the ends of the globe.

The scourge of generations, hate exterminates humankind,
decimates the innocent,
eradicates peace.

Its yawn is the dissolution of our common origin and bond,
enemy of human identity,
Armageddon of silence.

OPEN BORDERS

Relationship and understanding in place of decimation.
You stamp out a part of me, and a large slice of you falls out.
I am a part of you that you refuse to acknowledge,
branded by
accidentals.
Your borders are those of nations, ethnicity, and religion,
The artificial intelligence of humankind.
I am a part of your wholeness, just as you are of mine.
Why persist in knocking down every live stone
in this wall of humanity?
Why pursue silence when we're meant for voice and laughter?
Close the doors of fragmented hearts and minds.
Tear down the dividing walls.

ECOSYSTEM OF BURN

The hard, immovable rock lodged within
Moves into night, personage of my dreams.
Like Sisyphus, I feed it into blossoming
Tentacles, sapping the rationale,
The fiery blooms igniting my mind
A coat, impossible to shed grown into permanence.
Closest Companion by day
To live in its presence is the burning within.
My forest fire -
Merciless
Ravaging arteries and veins
Each corpuscle outmanned, chiseling joints, bulking muscles
The heart staked, pounded with the nails of "purity"
hands open to separation.
Stillness of voice, laughter, togetherness

LAMENT

October 7, 2023

The diaphanous wings of fireflies
burning torches in the huddle of night,
the honor guard, keeping vigil before the bloodletting.
A perfect welcome for royalty, spurned by stealth and jeer.
A home comfortably settled into the warmth of its routine.

You took the kibbutz with massive red.

Agony pouring down the face of yellowing plaster,
their heads hanging in shame.
Bellies punched out,
Grieving their defenseless survival.

A shield of quartz surely plated your mind,
blindfolded your tattooed heart.
frothy cells eclipsed the image of your grandmother,
holding you
in the warm embrace that only she had,
her serene smile flooding the furrows of her wise wrinkles,
Satiated from the celebration of her grandson's Bar Mitzvah.
kinship shattered by the arrogance of Dolomite.
A tender part of you severed, gone forever.

The credo erased the memory of your beloved son
As you thundered into the child's room
Into the arms of match box cars and trucks
Superman, Batman
The Legend of Zelda on the floor.
Your son, a breathless amalgam of the wadi
And of desert sands, tractor and bulldozer in hand
Face aglow as his eyes met yours.

Did your heart thaw in that minute?
Did your arm go limp?

A precious part of you, gone. Gone in a split second.

Did you hear your wife's voice?
Did you feel the touch of her soft hand within yours?
As she whispered, "What would I do without you?
What would life be like?
Hearts gone . . . gone forever.

Anesthesia wears off, melts the deep freeze, but with you,
every pore and cell are steeped in doctrine

The smile of permanence snatched with thawless talons.
The Crusader numbed . . .
Enslaved
Shackled . . .

The alarm clock persists in its shrill beeping.
Consternation over the silence of its wards.

The stove and the oven lament their exile in brutal territory,
While the milk and the eggs in the gaping mouth
of the refrigerator hold
their hands up high - in surrender.
The silver bicycle and the toy soldier bow down in remembrance.
The orphaned schoolhouse waits.

Is this how we leave, doused in the burn of hate?
Can you step onto the red carpet?

STYMIE

Words unspoken, saturating the silence of bodies,
Words unsaid, burning in raging embers
That sing a lullaby to the weighted columns
Announcing their glinting reign.

Words unsaid, burning in raging embers
Forbidden footprints molded into soil,
Announcing their glinting reign
Held close to the heart

Forbidden footprints molded into soil,
Lips and mouth, flowers of lead
Held close to the heart,
in dresses of virulent red
Daring to capture the brilliant hues

Flowers of lead, lips and mouth
Dripping in the dark wind
Daring to capture the brilliant hues
Mannequins statuesque in lifelessness

Dripping in the dark wind
Dust to dust, the consolation of lives stilled.
Mannequins statuesque in lifelessness
The incinerator of desecrated stalks

The consolation of lives stilled, dust to dust
Vociferous advocates of stories in scattered ash
The incinerator of desecrated stalks
Bulwarks of a blue sky.

Vociferous advocates of stories in scattered ash
Where the poppies shed their fragrance

Bulwarks of a blue sky
Saturating the silence of bodies in words unspoken.

Malala Yousafzai, a twelve-year-old girl from Pakistan, defied the Taliban and fought for the right to an education for Pakistani girls. On her way to school, she was shot in the head by the Taliban but miraculously survived this assassination attempt. She continues to speak out for women's rights throughout the world.

I AM MALALA

After Malala Yousafzai

Hush, my mother clamps her hand over my mouth.
The smells from the kitchen, the dough she's kneading
for *Parathas*
and the mutton infused in gravy on the earthen oven,
Smother my olfactory senses.
Hush, don't raise your voice!
You cannot and must not make yourself heard.
I knew I wasn't to have that privilege.
My *Ammi* made that clear. It was for the boys,
Only for the boys.
My unripened mind, soft as the lychees in my Swat Valley,
churns at this thought.
I know then - this is the very beginning of a cold, bitter, winter.
The kitchen has no warmth for you; my mind screams out–
The tingling of every organ clamors at this subjugation -
Yoked to reputation, honor, and respectability; straining
to breathe.

The air hangs low, weighing on me. "Are you sick, says *Ammi*?"
I take a deep breath, exhaling the heat within me
while the beads on my nose, upper lip and forehead grow
into a flood of resistance.

I feel the rough skin of *Ammi's* hand as she tries to smooth
the pain.
I lay my head against her breast, filled with her beating heart.
The
throbbing
now reaches greater proportions.
"No women teachers. All girls must stay home."
Femininity banned from school.

I droop in my burgeoning. Broken stems, fallen petals,
crushed one by one. The *Deodara* trees hold me hostage,
wrap their bristly claws around me,
make me one with those silenced by the Taliban,
Chained to my physicality while my mind cries out for mission.

Drooping flowers show their face once watered and fed. I must be
the nutrient injected into the soil of banned femininity.
Spines uncurl as the power of words, drowns the toxicity
of the oppressor, desperate to curb
the uprising of emboldened teens.

My brush with death; the shot in the head -
That's what it takes to restore feminine dignity
That's what it takes to restore the rights of girls to -
An education; to respectability.

The fragrance of the *Intifada* . . .

Machismo wilts in its overpowering scent.
That's what it takes - That's what it takes!

On Racial Superiority
Justification of oppression and cruelty

CHROMA

There's only one - Ebony on ivory.
They call it - iconic.
Black tresses, fair skin. They call it - stunning.
Universally accepted,
No matter what the language. It's always the same.
Quelle coiffure!
C'est magnifique!
Ebony on ivory
They call it - iconic.

That dark outfit!
That black dress!
It's a Dior!
Quel élégance!
La haute couture is wrapped in black
"*Mais pas Les Noirs*"
The subtleties are what counts,
Cementing the consciousness
Of generations.

Black sharps on white flats
Keys to melodious acceptance
Catalysts of peaceful interiors.
The mascara, the eyeliner, the sleek four-wheeler
Black accents on white.
They call it - iconic.

Ebony on Ebony. Ebony on coco
Loses all its flavor.
The aroma of cacao, drowned in the purity of stagnant hearts,
oblivious to insipid taste.
Minds arrested in tracks of worn paths,

afraid of braving the gusts
and the pelting of hail.

Are black and brown inherent repellants?
Immersing the being in the tar of repulsion?
Unlike the bees swarming to black on white,
as honey in the comb of appetite?
The one color in our palette,
The most savory is what we serve.
There - that's the difference!

ODE TO MOTHERS

Woman, you cradle the broken body
Crushed by a savage storm
Pelting hail into lifelessness.
Blood of your blood, your son.
You place him on the altar of sacrifice
Open to the sword,
In a sheath clothed in maternal grief
Known only to the one who gives birth.

I see these women, daughters of Eve
Embracing the flesh of their flesh
Inextricably meshed into a bloody shroud.
Shared suffering in this lineage of the garden
Waiting for sons and daughters to be crowned in glory.
I see lives destined for the killing fields,
Powered by a uniformed ego and the weapon.
Dismissing the unseen,
Incapable of comprehending the unspoken -

Rodney King: June 17, 2012
Eric Garner: July 17, 2014
Michael Brown: August 9, 2014
Freddie Gray: April 12, 2015
Sandra Bland: July 13, 2015
Philando Castile: July 6, 2016
Ahmaud Arbery: February 23, 2020
Breonna Taylor: March 13, 2020
George Floyd, May 25, 2020
Tyree Nichols: January 10, 2023

And . . . the hail flaunts its glinting steel,
while tears
water the silence.

Mother, you suffer and wait for the crown of martyrdom
How long for redemption?

Prototype of maternal sacrifice
Going back to the source

LA PIETÀ

After Michelangelo's sculpture : La Pietà

Tears wrapped in the folds of tender maternity
Grief buried in the arc of her head dress.
The gaze of her eyes lowered fixedly on the inert body enfolded
In the circle of her arms.
Mother, your love gushes unseen like the swell of an ocean
Saturating every pore of a lifeless shore,
Purifying the dried weed, salve of the hungry sand.
Mother, your peace washes every wound
On the body of your son
Lying in repose
Within the serenity of your embrace.
The tears of your heart pour out a dirge
Conjoined to the face of him who you bore.
Returned to you now, as the curve of your hands
Contemplates the two-edged sword of his destiny
in surrendered offering.

Mother, you are the pillar, nestling the head
which your footsteps sought.
His hands and his feet find their resting place
in your seamless mantle
As he is now offered to you.

Societal Pressure
Crowd mentality inciting violence

DO I BELIEVE?

Your face reflects the one who made me,
The blood in your veins is, as pure as mine?
Do I believe that you feel pain, that you gnaw on hurts that have
grown roots?
That you breathe the same emotions I do?
Do I believe that the equality of humankind is an abstraction,
Penned in a proclamation far from what I see?

Slogans, banners, signs in large letters, screaming the equality
of all humankind,
Is this lip service? Are these externals meant to *show* that I care?
Do I ask myself with the honesty that goes beyond,
and that looks within -
Do I believe?
Will I give up my all for a stranger, or is this but a ploy to fit in?
Am I proclaiming my virtue, or do these deeds emanate
from true conviction?
Seated in the heart and in the soul, in the very depths
of my being? Does my heart expand with unlimited room
to be welcoming and accepting?

As Wave upon wave surges into the streets
And Chants roll into impassioned speech . . .
Do they believe? Is this veracity or contagion?
A desire to melt into the crowd?
Do I let the chains fall from my heart
Do I set the caged particles free?

What is the flavor of my life?
What is the spice that fires up my every day?
Let this not be a singular, one time participation
But a mission that's an integral part of me.

Never losing its flavor.
Do I attune my ear
To listen to the small still voice within me whisper –
We are all the beautiful faces of a shared humanity
You are the beloved
Just as I am

PLUMB THE DEPTHS

We carry within ourselves, the ancestral home, stately, righteous,
budding with the seeds of Destruction
Grown into rock, stratum of the soul.
We neglect the fields of our being, letting the weeds
grow rampant, into oaks of Injustice and Oppression.
Putting off to another day, the dagger of hate polluting
the blood.
Immovable in smugness, refusing to face the plaque, strategizing
within our arteries.
The Honey Suckle blossoms into orange, soothing
to the eye,
camouflaging the purity of creation over which it tramples,
pushing origin deeper into a bottomless pit in which
There is no survival.
It smothers and suffocates the breath of oneness.
Our hearts are girdled into establishment digging its
parasitic roots into our foundation
Weaving its pronged horns into lenses clouded over by
the cataracts
of
time which normalizes the tartar hardened into cement.
Denying the scalpel – the malignancy of centuries old
brick,
dodging the abrasion of pulling off the adhesive - skin,
raw in its refusal to
face and to acknowledge the darkness within.
We flow downstream, one among the shoal . . . unnoticed,
secure . . .
Avoiding the arduous trek upstream, a lone warrior
taking on the forces of Animosity and Bigotry.
I watch callused hands chiseling the mortar, piece by
piece,

submerged in a steady stream of crumbled debris.
The bent back digs out the boulders, aligns the brick,
takes back
each crevice captured by poison ivy.
The promise of the salve

DREAM/REALITY

The subliminal wheat cultivated in dreams, succumbs
to the kaleidoscope of hibernation. A landscape of bare branches
withering from existence.

The first chapter - An ache that cleaves to the pit of the stomach.
The migraine of unfulfilled desire.
The tenement, the vermin, the rats cushioned into the pillow
of my neck, warm as the burlap over me.
I walk past the schoolhouse, feet planted before the eateries, stare
of a robot, eyeing the flies, those pesky creatures, buzzing
over the sugary creations. I'm in full view of the *mithai wala*.
There's a spark there.

On the threshold of the second chapter - Bondage of
heart and mind.
My heart escapes, only to be caged. Mind and body
follow the fugue. The heart flies out of the hutment.
Physicality on firm ground. The roaches scramble up bare feet.
Exposed, panicked, scurrying for the nooks and crannies
that can't be found. Bleeding cracks on soles provide no solace,
no hermitage for varmints!

I follow into the land of tinsel. Crushed and broken by the weight
of a forked tongue. The body distanced from the tenement,
under a barrage of shifty eyes and groping hands. Exposed -
An arena of glaring spotlights, a wobbly, makeshift stage,
hands without limits. A pit of
envy.
Huis Clos is my destiny. A hollowed-out heart, floundering
in a river of red while the hammer pounds the flesh. A body
cringing, corralled, dripping with the iron of the horseshoe.

My brand has no choice. I am the dancing *Tamasha* girl . . .
Tamasha girl . . . *Tamasha* girl . . .

Stigma
The branding of birth

TOUCH

Among your own, to be shamed.
You are of the Dravidian race.
I know what that means.
You ousted me, never to look up,
To know I never belonged,
Never would.
My presence was a nebulous absence
A shadow, hand in hand with darkness.
Days as a nocturnal bat
A moth swatted ...
Until you came and gave me an identity.
My wallpaper more than scabbed over, dried the bleeding, tearing
the heart; covered my pockmarked soul
After years of carrying it around my neck,
Yoked to me with an iron clad chain.

The bag of sighs, of moans tightly shut, of sobs stifled
underfoot released, fled to their escape
Prisoners of liberation

THE FIRE INSIDE

I've climbed the mountain of insults
I've turned the other cheek
Knowing I am no better than the one who mocks
The one who spits into my face -
But no worse.
It takes courage to resist and not
Fight back in the same
Way you've been treated.

It takes self-knowledge
To know who you are; to know where you come from . . .

To know I'm loved by the one who matters,
The one who is true help and true hope.
This is our bloodless revolution
Where all rise to life!
Why mete out what we've been subjected to?

Giving without counting the cost
Going against the grain

HUNGER

A forgotten rag. At first, carefully chosen, sought out from among
the others sporting their well-polished surfaces,
placed strategically on the
shelf.
This one needed to be special, rather unique,
to stand the test of being
squeezed, giving up every fiber in the body.
Every pore and cell engaged in the combat of giving
without thinking for
a moment of holding back.
Giving to the last drop. Never the dry stream.
Gurgling not gasping.

Sacrifice. What does the word hold?

Instilling self-esteem in those who are oppressed
Lifting up the ostracized

PUT ON DIGNITY

After Mariotto Albertinelli's painting: Visitation

Maiden adorned in royal blue
Infinity shines down upon you
in the smile of the open skies.
O bearer of eternity,
Gateway of transcendence,
The ornate arch carries your stately stature,
and
Bows in reverence,
O doorway to heaven.

Your cousin, a daughter of Aaron, holds you
In honor of an inter-generational embrace.
Her eyes behold your posture of prayer
As with lowered head and eyes in worship
You ponder and reflect on the miracle within you.

O mother of God and of humanity,
Your cousin marvels at your generosity.
Carrying divinity within you,
You die to self, in service of the one who has borne
the
shame of barren age.
The power of your presence
Resurrects her gnarled hands and resigned heart
With vigor and hope.
The embers of life have been set ablaze,
As her son, the greatest born of woman
Acknowledges the one you carry, as Savior and Lord.

CATHARSIS

To be loved, no matter who you are.
To be loved, because you are.
The homeless, the beggar, the abandoned
on the street corner or huddled in the confines of a dank refuge.
Skeletal frame of a once "furry" friend pretzeled against a sparse
twig,
The only one who dares to warm the refuse and ignite
an inseparable heat.

A sigh at the touch. This is all he yearns for -
Shadow's offering.
Streaming rivulets among sunken chasms wiped clean
with an assiduous tongue.
The nudge of a wet nose opening the palm of the twig,
crisscrossed by
the cruelties of time.
A life surrendered to addiction.
A presentation of crags and a skeletal frame, the best friend
elicits a smile
on lips parched, torn and beaten down.
The paws stroke the bony frame, fountain of well-being,
benefactor.

It's life in the giving and receiving. Without conditions.
Stoking the warmth, streaming into the well-formed stalactites,
craving food and shelter.
More energizing and intense than the roaring fire
in that family room-
Ornate mantle, inhabited by the smiling faces of children
in gilded picture frames,
a leather backed couch,
the gentleman

in the recesses
of
a plush recliner.
The icicles of abandonment overflow . . .